Affirm Your Worth
The Change You Own

30 Days of Positive Af-firmations

All Rights Reserved

This publication is copyright protected and is intended for personal use only. No part of this publication may be altered or reproduced in any form or by any means, electronic, mechanical, photocopying, recording or otherwise transmitted, without express written permission from the author.

This book is for informational purposes only and no parts should be considered as medical advice. You must not rely on the information in this publication as a substitute to advice from a medical professional such as your doctor or other professional health care provider.

This book is for informational purposes only, and no warranties of any kind are expressed or implied. Although every precaution has been taken in the preparation of this work, neither the author, publisher, affiliates or partners shall have any liability to any personal or entity with respect to any loss or damage caused or alleged to be caused directly or indirectly by the information contained in this book. Readers acknowledge that the author is not offering legal, financial, medical or professional advice.

www.drafriyierandle.com

Copyright © 2018   Dr. Afriyie Randle

This book is dedicated to my wonderful daughter Logan Alise, my always supportive mother, brother and a host a family, friends and associates. Thank you all for depositing love, encouragement, and solace at the appointed times. My passion to share affirmations is driven by the continuous support of the aforementioned. I will always put positivity into the universe as every being has greatness in them and must all be reminded through positive affirmations.

Forward

I first met Dr. Afriyie Randle when we were both Resident physicians at St. Joseph's Hospital, North Philadelphia Hospital System, Philadelphia, PA. We were both single parents absolutely in love with our children and absolutely determined to become licensed physicians, medical professionals on a mission, to be of service and to change the world for the better. We worked hard, we studied together, we learned how to take care of patients as we accompanied each other on hospital rounds, we cried, we laughed, we talked about our kids, our love lives, our bills, and most importantly our hopes and dreams. We even became Chief Residents together, splitting up the responsibilities so we could continue to tend to our parenting responsibilities. And yes, we also struggled together. At times this realizing our dream of becoming physicians seemed all uphill with endless requirements to complete our training, licensing exams, senior research to complete, rotations to arrange and complete. It was during a particularly challenging time time that I came up with what soon became our mantra: Faith, Focus, Finish! It became a collective affirmation that calmed the rough seas of the calamity of graduate medical education. It became the reminder that individually and collectively we were daughters of our faith, that we were highly intelligent and were endowed with not only strength of mind but we were also courageous and could therefore focus, and finally as each task presented itself there was only one thing we could do and that was to finish! I was and forever will be deeply honored by having been asked to write the forward for Dr. Afriyie's book on affirmations. When Dr. Afriyie told me that she was writing a book on affirmations, I couldn't help but reflect back on our Faith, Focus, and Finish. She also shared that the reason for the book was that these self penned affirmations became the breadcrumbs to her soul as she followed their path to remain true to herself in the face of some daunting challenges both professional and personal. I am deeply moved by the fact that Dr. Afriyie wants to share her affirmations with the rest of us knowing that if something breaks through the reader's defenses, sadness, loneliness, self doubt, and, disappointment, loneliness or what ever may be holding them back then that person also has an opportunity to heal, to grow, to be strengthened and be made whole again. It is understood from our scientific literature that affirmations have benefits across threatening situations; affirmations can decrease stress, increase well being, improve academic performance and make people more open to behavior change [Cohen and Sherman (2014)]. Whatever Dr. Afriyie does she does with purpose and passion, I for one, know that just as these affirmations have changed her life these pearls of her wisdom will change your life too.

Dr. Carol Penn, DO, Dipl. ABOM, MA, FACCE
www.drcarolpenn.com
Faculty, Center for Mind Body Medicine Clinical Faculty Rowan University School of Osteopathic Medicine

Contents

DAY 01
I am the best version of me — 9

DAY 02
I define myself. I fit my mold — 11

DAY 03
I am enough. I refuse to be treated less than what I'm worth — 12

DAY 04
I am worthy of love and deserve the best love has to offer without conditions — 14

DAY 05
My past doesn't define who I am — 15

DAY 06
I define who I am — 17

DAY 07
I will not be captive to my emotions or myself — 18

DAY 08
I am not inferior because of the choices I've made — 20

DAY 09
I trust myself to make better decisions concerning my life — 21

DAY 10
I will choose my company wisely — 23

DAY 11
The voice inside my head isn't always right — 25

DAY 12
I won't be a slave to someone's perception of me. It's their issue to contend with — 27

DAY 13
I will no longer fear losing someone who is treating me poorly   28

DAY 14
I won't look at saying no or setting boundaries as a form of disclusion but as a decision of CHOOSING ME   30

DAY 15
I love my imperfections   31

DAY 16
I am confident   32

DAY 17
I am beautiful   33

DAY 18
I am strong   35

DAY 19
I am faithful   36

DAY 20
I love myself   37

DAY 21
I have peace of mind   38

DAY 22
I am positive a force   40

DAY 23
I attract positivity   41

DAY 24
I am whole   42

DAY 25
I am no longer wounded   43

DAY 26
I am the status quo   44

DAY 27
I trust my knowing   46

DAY 28
I'm my own person   47

DAY 29
I'm above average   48

DAY 30
I accept my greatness   49

DAY 01

I am the best version of me

It is becoming extremely difficult for us to refuse the peer pressure of society. Never in human history have we been this connected. Thanks to the internet, your circle of influence increases with each like, follow and retweet.

Social media has refined our understanding of the world. Today, people can quickly gather to create movements for positive change, which is a tremendous leap for mankind. But, all this positivity comes at a steep price.

Countless studies have shown that the more connected we get, the less intuitive we become. Many people are losing their sense of value. Discovering your inner self is now a lost art: we depend on the media to interpret everything because we've forgotten that we are the best decision makers on this planet.

To truly enjoy your life and uncover all your hidden potentials, you must be in tune with your inner self. You must believe that you are the best at what you do and no else can be you.

You are more than what the naysayers think. Take a moment to dive into your thoughts and you will unlock mysteries about yourselves. Have you heard about a woman name Mary Jane McLeod Bethune, if not, maybe you've heard of our 32nd preseindent Franklin D. Roosevelt. Bethune was appointed as a national advisor to Roosevelt to what was known as the his "Black Cabinet". She offered guidance to Roosevelt on the concerns of blacks. She was born to slave parents and at an early age took an interest in education. Later Bethune used $1.50 to start the Educational and Industrial Training School for Negro Girls which is now known today at Bethun-Cookman College.

You must become your greatest cheerleader if you want to make your dreams a reality. Bethune was faced with many obstacles. Despite this she became known as "The First Lady of The Struggle". Bethune a humanitarian, civil rights activist, and educator who has touched so many lives through her College alone.

Take control by standing up for yourself. The world is full of self-made victims, you can live above the struggle if only you believe that you are the best version of yourself. Commit to your dreams: belief, be willing to do what it takes to become the best and in time your goals will become a reality.

Believing in yourself is not optional. Don't get weighed down by doubt, believe that you can pull through the hard times. Remember that you are the only one that sees that grand vision. Believe and you will achieve irrespective of the negativity.

DAY 02

I define myself.
I fit my mold

No one is born with a complete certainty of who they are to become. You choose who you want to be. You create your reality, one that no one else has any right force upon you. Despite our freedom to choose many still fall prey to the heavy pressures of society's opinion.

Life is a beautiful journey, uncovering the path you designed by yourself is the greatest achievement anyone can have. This truth is what makes Steve Jobs story stands out amongst others. Steve never wanted to start a consumer computer company since the day he was born.

No, he discovered his passions and identified an opportunity to positively impact the world through Apple.Inc. Don't give up your liberty. Be aware that everyone including your parents, spouse, and loved ones are actively trying to mold you into their vision. If you give them the opportunity, you will only become a figment of someone else's imagination.

You are more than capable of choosing your own life. Don't let anyone tell you your dreams are worthless or that you have no right to define your own reality. You are no longer a slave to society, be mindful because your freedom came at a great cost.

A few setbacks are nothing to worry about because we have to try multiple times before we find the right career, soul mate, and job that suits us. I was once told by one of my beloved college professors that I should try a different career after not being accepted into medical school the fist time I applied, but here I am today a physician thriving in my destined path. Let every decision you make be from a place of value which you choose.

You are free to decide to be moral, to be friendly, be loving and do the things that make you happy. We are all born a blank slate, only those who take the initiative will truly live out their dreams while others are left behind to become followers.

DAY 03

I am enough. I refuse to be treated less than what I'm worth

Take a moment to think deeply about the following statements:

I've invested years despising my brain, for the way it moves and changes and never remains the same, never maintains a similar core interest. It wasn't adequate.

I've invested years despising my heart, for aching when I don't need it to, and leading me in the most noticeably awful conceivable path. It wasn't adequate.

I've invested years detesting my stance, recollecting how individuals used to ridicule me for it, trying to belittle me. It wasn't adequate.

I've invested years hating my abilities and my gifts. I felt they were not and could never be sufficient. It wasn't adequate.

I've invested years despising my body. The way it looks, the way it moves. The way I treat it, and the way it treats me back. It wasn't adequate.

I've invested years despising whatever parts of my identity make it so difficult for me to reach my goals. It wasn't adequate.

I've invested years despising the piece of me that resents others, that draws on it and feeds off it. It wasn't adequate.

I've invested years despising my clothes, the things I possess, the things I do. It wasn't adequate.

If you relate to any of these statements, then it is time for a change. You have had enough self-hate for one lifetime. From now on you refuse to be treated less than what you are worth.

You are not a door mat for others to step on, you are not here just to make other people happy. You deserve a chance to be yourself. You deserve the rewards for what you've rightfully earned.

No longer will anyone make you feel guilty for their emotions, no longer will you sit quietly while toxic people ride on your kind heart. Your voice deserves to be heard, your opinions matter, you have a right to be forgiven when you make mistakes. Above all, you deserve the right to be happy.

DAY 04

I am worthy of love and deserve the best love has to offer without conditions

The choice of who we love and how we love them is personal. Opening your heart to people is not a sign of weakness but a proof of strength. Love despite is something we all deserve. Too many people make the mistake of assuming that giving their all will lead to a reciprocation of their love.

Be mindful of who you build connections with because humans are susceptible to abusing good people. Sometimes we ignore our needs just to make others feel comfortable, most times we hide our visionsand dreams out of concernthat it may offend those we say we love. But in a sad twist of fate, they, the ones who are supposed to love us unconditionally may take us for granted.

Dread is an offensive word. It keeps us from pure bliss. We abstain from anything that is agonizing, even though continuing taking the neglect in the present circumstance harms us more. All we want is to be loved for our true selves, yet we hide this deep desire for fear of being left alone when we ask for the what we deserve.

You need to discover for yourself that it is okay if people do not like you. The real individuals who are supposed to be in your life will be attracted to you when you are yourself. Guess what, the connection you build with those who love you will stand the test of time. If only you take back control of your heart and let the narcissistic people go.

Have a limit and let them know that you too deserve love. If they refuse, be brave: move on. The game of love is a tactical one, sometimes you lose and sometimes you win. Do not be afraid to lose the people who will not make sacrifices for you. Don't be afraid to lose the people who never see your value. They speak negativity into your life, they always try to make you feel less than and they actively try to sabotage anything that makes you happy. This person could be a parent, child, spouse, or friends.

Don't be like a toy vessel being hurled about in the sea, it is a depleting experience. Feel free to open your heart to love and give yourself permission to be loved too.

DAY 05

My past doesn't define who I am

This may seem confusing to you but when you understand that you have power over the past, you will overcome. It is hard to teach people that their past does not define who they are because we are nothing without our memories.

Have you ever met someone suffering from memory loss or dementia? If you have, the first thing you'll notice is a change in their personality. Without memories, we lose ourselves. Why then should you not value yourself through the eyes of the past?

This question has lingered in the mind of many for decades, and some confuse the meaning of letting go of the past as forgetting what happened. That is not the real truth. Never forget what happened: nature designed us to remember negative encounters more because it threatens our survival.

Your anxieties, phobias and painful memories are no coincidence. The goal is not to forget but to serve as emotional reminders and insight on how to proceed. No matter how hard we try, we cannot control everything that happens to us especially during our childhoods.

What we can do is to not allow this experience to define our future. Emotions are only there to guide you. Yes, I know they are important and they tell a true story, but you want to use your pain to move ahead. Don't let the past sink your future. You can defeat the thoughts if you believe that you can.

Oprah Winfrey the famous TV mogul tells of the experiences she sufferd as a child being raped and molested robbed her of a childhood. Still, she credits these experiences with her zeal to succeed and be empathetic toawards others. You too can do this. The past has happened, learn from it, don't dwell in it.

When you continually focus your mind in the past, it exaggerates the pain you feel. Also dwelling on the past limits your ability to truly appreciate your capacities. Ryan Stewman went to jail twice, got divorced, lost all his money, but he knew he is not a looser or just an ex-convict.

He picked up himself and created a profitable real estate sales business. No matter how painful the memory is, don't give your past the power of defining your identity.

The hardest reality for most people to deal with is that despite the fact that your past experiences are painful: It challenges all we know, driving us out of our comfort zones into a brave new world of positive change.

DAY 06

I define who I am

Democratic, Liberal or Republican? Black, White, or other? Homosexual, Heterosexual or Bisexeual? Christian, Muslim, or Atheist? These are the common questions we as Americans ask ourselves all the time. But have you ever thought about why people like tagging themselves?

Humans are designed to defend themselves by tags. It could be your career, spiritual or political beliefs. By doing this we fail to see the individual and promote group thinking instead. Studies show that we make bad irrational decisions when we are in groups. We lose our sense of direction to the group identity and we forget that we, the individual is important.

Don't allow people to define you with tags. This is a sign of lazy thinking. Mature minds know that the law of averages does not apply to real issues. When you see your self only by the names society call you, then you will limit yourself.

You lose your identity; your sense of selfworth will slowly erode. You must take charge and only define your identity by what you believe. You are not an idea, you are a living being adapting to the changes that you face daily.

In his early years of politics, the 44th president of America, Barack Hussein Obama was caught on camera saying he does not believe in gay rights, but years later he joined forces to fight with the oppressed helping them gain their liberty.

You too might strongly believe in something today, then change your mind the next day. It does not make you a hypocrite. I know too many people who place themselves in a box and reject any help because they are worried about what others will think.

Be comfortable in your own skin. If you decide to redefine yourself then do it, because you are in charge of your identity. To your greatest surprise the people who truly love you will accept you for who you are.

DAY 07
I will not be captive to my emotions or myself

From the dawn of time, we have always been driven by our feelings. As our world became more complex, so did our feelings. Access to vast amounts of information is a good thing but if you are emotionally reckless, this will overwhelm you.

During my medical residency I learned to trust my gut. It can be quite difficult to make a snap judgment that could lead to someone living or someone dying. Most times we ignore our gut feelings and do the wrong thing because we want to impress people who most likely do not care about us. We hide our terrible feelings because we don't want to be judged for not being a team player or thinking outside the box.

The real problem is not that we have these emotions or that we have mastered the art of pretense: the issue lies with why we have those feelings in the first place. If you meet someone for the first time and you feel a sense of distrust, something must have triggered you. Your emotions are guides, to help you navigate the difficulty of being alive.

You need your emotions but to be truly free, you must not be a slave to it. Dan Goleman in his 1996 book "Emotional Intelligence" explains that people who cannot manage their emotions will be subject to the mercy of those who can. Your emotions can drive you to success or pull you towards failure. The goal is to manage your feelings.

Understand why you feel what you feel. Why don't you trust that person? Why is your stomach acting up whenever you go to visit your parents? I am sorry to inform you that you cannot hide your emotions forever. It will only be bottled up and spring out like a caged monster if you don't come to terms with it.

Don't be afraid of how you feel, your mind is only trying to tell you something. Listen to it, acknowledge how you feel. Respect your reactions, stop being a tyrant to yourself, and show self compassion. When you disrespect your feelings, you slowly become a bitter, jealous, and negative person. Emotions are not meant to be hidden, they are supposed to be expressed.

Sometimes you may need to take direct action while other times all you need to do is agree that you feel the way you do; the secret is to be in charge of the decision making. When you do this, you will no longer be a hostage to the contemplations of your body, allowing you to experience the freedom to be.

DAY 08

I am not inferior because of the choices I've made

Perfection is just an illusion of reality that often hinders us from reaching our truest potential. We all want to appear flawless, so no one will judge us. So many people are afraid of taking risks and doing the things they truly want to do because of fear of that awkward feelings. When we tell someone about our choices and things go wrong, we fear the feeling of failure.

However, it's not just failure we fear, we fear to lose our money, losing trust, being confronted that we were unable to do what we said we could do. Deeprooted fear denies many their dream life. My mother would call these deeprooted fears "dream thieves".

To achieve success, you must learn that you are beyond your choices. Yes, we make thousands of decisions every day, the good news is that there is always a new day to change.

Richard Branson, one of the most successful entrepreneurs of all time openly admitted his defeat when he said: "I'll never again make the mistake of thinking that all large, dominant companies are sleepy!".

He made the mistake of starting Virgin Cola both in the UK and US, the business failed within ten years. He could have let that one mistake define his empire, but he did not. He kept trying new products and ideas. Today, Richard is directly competing with Elon Musk and Jeff Bezos in the space exploration industry.

It is okay to admit that you have made a bad decision, let go of the idea of being perfect and embrace your flaws. Don't put yourself down when others praise you for your hard work, don't be afraid to have some scares. If you try too hard, you will either play the blame game or you'll quit. Don't do it.

Avoid blaming others and avoid being too hard on yourself. Whenever you made a choice that leads to a less than expected outcome, don't give up! Learn from it and move on because if you dwell too much on it, you will become a victim of your own making

DAY 09
I trust myself to make better decisions concerning my life

Deciding to choose a career in medicine was definitely a difficult one for me. It came with terrain that was often difficult to navigate. Studies show that on average, we (adults) make over 10,000 decisions every single day. Despite the fact that we are familiar with making decisions, it is still one of the hardest skills for many to master. Yes, we make a lot of small unnoticeable decisions but it's our subconscious mind that does the bulk of the work.

Therefore, when we need to make the big decisions like starting a business or where to live, it seems hard. Most people will openly admit to being slow decision makers and many ends up doubting the decisions they make.

This is a major problem when you turn 18, you are now expected to choose wisely. The reality of your life will be greatly determined by the decisions you make. You must learn to be confident that you made the right choices.

And, even when it goes wrong, learn and make better decisions next time. Don't throw yourself under the city bus because you've made a wrong decision. I always encourage people to seek the counsel of others for important life decisions, but you must not limit yourself to their words. Take it into account as what it is, advice.

If you want to be free and live the life you dream of then you must be in charge of your own decision making, no matter how dificult it may seem to you. The more you learn to trust your decisions, the better you'll get.

Don't rely too much on others as you may have insights and passion that they don't. During the founding years of Walmart, Sam Walton decided to focus is attention on gathering data on what's selling and what does not.

He achieved this by holding weekly employee meetings, asking for insights he was not aware of. Today, Walmart stores earned over $482 billion in revenue between 2012 and 2018. Remember that this was in the 1960s, long before the internet, online stores and of course there were no tracking AI.

Even though other businesses were not taking this approach, Sam decided to invest his time in understanding his customers which paid off big time. If you cannot make simple decisions in your life, then how do you expect to handle a business, family, career or even a relationship?

It may take a long time and some errors, but you must believe, trust that you can make good decisions. Don't be afraid of what may go wrong, focus your attention on what will go right. Refusing to decide is also a decision.

You cannot run away from your life because your lack of decisiveness will make you miss many opportunities creating regrets. Take it heads on. You can do it. You are either in control of yourself or someone else is.

If there is one skill that you must learn to become a happy and successful person, then it must be decision making. Take the initiative, calm the storm inside and trust that you are good enough to make the best decisions in every area of your life.

DAY 10
I will choose my company wisely

Ever heard this quote "A mirror reflects a man's face, but what he is really like is shown by the kind of friends he chooses." By Colin Powel? He is spot on; the company you keep reflects who you are.

If you spend too much time with them, it begins to affect you too. The age-old saying of you show me your friends and I will tell you who you are is exactly all you need to understand about good company.

Sad people like to hang around other sad people, and bright minds enjoy being with each other. That is just the way things are. Don't make that excuse, you do not have to be with that abusive parent or spouse. They don't need you to soak up all their negativity. Sometimes we act nice because we do not want to hurt other people's feelings, but they do not care about your feelings.

If you keep listening to negative people, they assume that you enjoy their rants. And the depressing truth is that maybe you do. Because if you don't why do you condone it. Be careful who you spend time with, be careful of your inner circle as these people have great influence over you.

It can be very difficult to choose your friends because we as a society believe that people just walk into our lives. We are born into a family, we just naturally had friends and without much thought, we fall hopelessly in love. It feels wrong to be picky, don't allow your feeling to deceive you. You can't choose family, everybody else you can choose.

You have a choice of who comes into your life and when to let go of the toxic ones. I had a childhood friend with whom I got into trouble with all the time. We were always somewhere we shouldn't have been. My mother and brother taught me with "if she jumped off a bridge would you do it to". The funny thing is it wasn't my friend's company that caused vexation. It was as Captain Planet would say "our powers combined" that was the true issue. When we were in the company of each other we created and lived a life of mischief. As a young adolescence I had to choose better for myself and as fates would have it, we separated.

What is needed in your life is people who see the vision, people who are willing to go the extra mile for you and be there for in your darkest times. Take a moment to evaluate your company, become conscious and believe that you have what it takes to choose the right company.

DAY 11
The voice inside my head isn't always right

There is one thing you need to always be aware of, and that is we, humans are built to survive. We are continuing to adapt to modern civilization. Society is changing at a pace that is making it dificult for our biology to catch up. This is the most important reason why so many of us feel out of place most times.

If you suffer from depression, mood swings, and suicidal ideations, you are not alone. The world health organization (WHO), lists depression as one of the leading cause of ill health and disability worldwide. The reason for such rising stats is that we are not used to being in control of what happens inside of us, and no one is teaching us how to.

You need to take charge of your thoughts because if you don't it will consume you. It's not sensible to ignore the voice in your head, it is very dangerous to constantly try to control it. You need to listen. What is the voice telling you? Is it an issue you need to pay attention to?

The voice in our head acts as a guide for predicting the future and helping us avoid a negative experience. The problem is that most people confuse these expectations with reality, It is not. You decide what the reality is. The way to go about it is to notice when the voice is acting up. Try to discuss with it. If you are lucky, it will explain why it's acting up.

At this point, you'll need to give the real feedback. A common example is when people go for a job interview, many are nervous because it's an emotional experience. Someone is judging your every move, if you say something they perceive as wrong you might lose a great opportunity.

So, in this scenario, there's a lot at stake here. The proven method for a job interview is to calm down, avoid the pressure of being late and tell the voice that things will turn out like they are suppose to.

This is true for many situations when the voice is going bizarre, repeat it to yourself what the true reality is. Tell yourself that whatever is unnerving you is not the end of the world. Don't be afraid, that voice is yours. Speak to it with boldness and it will remain calm.

DAY 12

I won't be a slave to someone's perception of me. It's their issue to contend with

How often do you find yourself judging people you don't know? I bet the answer is almost every day. Your mind is constantly assigning roles and features to everything and everyone based on your experiences. What you think about someone may not be true, but the mind has a way of persuading us that it the only option.

The phenomenon of judging people without facts is a big problem in modern society as it creates strife in the community. The age of information and social media increases the difficulty of learning to understand before judging. So, don't expect people not to judge you, they will. It is how you handle the words and attitudes that matter.

You can try as hard as you want people are stubborn, even when they know the truth, they might still have a wrong perception of you and your dreams. Despite the fact that Katherine Johnson mathmetician for NASA ultimately was recognized on the big sceen by director Theodore Melfi's Hidden Figures and awarded the Presidential Medal of Freedom in 2015 for her relentless work analyzing and calculating space flights she was first thought as incapable based on the sterotypes of the time.

People remember negative things more than positive events. You could be the nicest person in the world, just one day of misunderstanding and your reputation will be ruined. Give up trying to please people.

That is why you must avoid being dependent on the opinions of others. You are on a journey called life, uncovering yourself each day. You do not want to live by another's opinion. They don't know what's going on inside, they have no idea how you feel. Even if you tell them your dreams, they still might not get it.

You too can reshape your life and achieve your goals, if only you let go of the phrase "what will people think of me". Know that you are not responsible for what others think and feel. Your emotions are your priorities, let them deal with theirs.

DAY 13

I will no longer fear losing someone who is treating me poorly

The damage of fear of uncertainty is created in all of us as children. Society teaches us early to be very cautious about what might happen, to avoid anything that could lead to unpleasant outcomes. We go through life avoiding confrontations with people because we are afraid that no one will like us.

The fear of being alone is a driving force behind why so many put up with toxic people. We constantly search for validation from others even when they ignore us. I know the thought of having no one to share our precious moments with is scary, but you must hold on to yourself.

There are over seven billion people alive currently on planet earth and yet we feel only that there is only one person can bring joy to our hearts, while there are many. There are individuals that serve different purposes in your life. There's someone out there craving your attention. Someone special desperately searching for your presence. Yet, you keep holding on to the ones who has no value for you. Repeat the following statements to yourself:

I am a valuable person

I am worth the attention

I am worthy of love

I acknowledge that I am afraid of losing him/her, but I am sure I will survive this.

I am not alone, I will never be alone.

The problem is that we mix up being alone with loneliness. We dread hearing our own minds thrive. We constantly look for people to fill a non-existent void. The key is to get used to being alone. No one is perfect; however, this is not an excuse to condone bad treatment from others.

The way out is taking regular breaks from the stress of everyday life to enjoy your own presence. People will always come and go, it's inevitable. Your best chance of getting it right is trusting that you can depend on you. Be that amazing person that is not half full but one who is complete by themselves.

DAY 14

I won't look at saying no or setting boundaries as a form of disclusion but as a decision of CHOOSING ME

Do you know that never saying no to the request of others may be symptoms of physiological disorder? It's called dependent personality disorder. One with this disorder has a fear of being alone, abandoned or seperated from people. Perhaps you may suffer from this form of mental illness and for this I advise you to go to your health care provider. Or, you may suffer from People Pleaser Syndrome. This is such a big issue for society because we consider people who are always available and willing to do the extra work to be nice.

A team player are what they call these people who never say no to the boss when he is asked to work overtime. The corporate world loves such people, they are sometimes masked as employees of the month.

There is so much we have to deal with today: work, life, kids, parents, siblings, colleagues, neighbors and even politics. Without limits, you cannot properly schedule your time. you need to know that irrespective of your view, boundaries exist. If you do not enforce them, then other people, your body or nature will.

Successful people are very disciplined with their resources because they know how valuable they are. You need time to rest, be with your family, have fun, and focus on building your dream. In order for you to have time for this, you must deliberately learn the art of saying No. When people try to manipulate you, say No.

When people try to make you feel guilty for their own problems, say no. When people try to call you selfish for looking out for your own interest, say No. Only take on task because you choose to not because you are obligated to.

Play your role in your life, family, and work but refuse to be the fool that others come to when they fail to do their own work. Be bold: it will be hard, eventually, that negative feeling of guilt will fade away.

DAY 15
I love my imperfections

Your flaws make you who you are, nobody else on the planet can ever be you. Perfectionism is an idealistic state of being based on what your perception of all things good.

It's okay to improve yourself but it's a very miserable experience to always try to be perfect. Everyone has flaws that are a part of our identity: you would not be human is there wasn't anything odd about you.

Lance Armstrong one of the most beloved athletics of our time tarnished his career because he desperately tried to maintain his perfect persona. The world would have still celebrated him if he settles for finishing a race after he survived cancer.

But no, he insisted on being the ultrachampion with a happy marriage and perfect family. He lost it all, now history remembers him as one of the cyclists who cheated.

Perfectionist find it difficult to see others win, they always want to be the best at everything which is not possible. They won't turn it into a Frozen moment and just "Let it go". You are amazing no doubt, being perfect is not realistic. Don't worry about it rather focus on the things you can change instead of the ones you can't.

When you focus on what is in your control, you'll find happiness. When you try too hard to bend the world to your will, then you will pay a great price for it. Remind yourself that it is okay to have flaws. You are good enough which is an achievement on its own.

Be content with who you are, even though the media keeps trying to sell us the idea of perfection to incite our greed, it's not that important. Believe it or not, no one likes to be with a perfect person. Be yourself. There's no shame in being you.

DAY 16

I am confident

Self-confidence is the Key to Success, without it you lack the will to take massive efforts which leads to great outcomes. While some people have natural selfconfidence, others don't. This should not bother you as the belief in one's ability can be learned.

I don't subscribe to the "fake it till you make it" saying. I believe that we all at one point or the other in our lives will doubt our abilities,. The most powerful way I have found to deal with misfortunes is positive thinking. Thomas Edison, the US inventor with over 1,093 patents to his name was once told by his teacher that he is too stupid to succeed.

Yet, he embraced the reality and kept working at it. Edison continued working on his electricity experiments even after he failed 9,000 times. This is the foundation of confidence. Helen Keller once said, "Positive thinking is the confidence that prompts accomplishment". Whenever you find yourself in doubt, believe and practice.

The repetition of the action will build you from the inside. Oprah Winfrey was fired from her job because she was unfit for TV but she did not give up. She kept at it until she became a TV icon, influencing minds all over the world. Don't let anything or anyone get in your way. For life to be meaningful you need hope, and without confidence, you can't achieve the extraordinary. You can get it done if you keep trying. Remember that winners are losers who never gave up.

Be your own ally, trust that what you have to offer is superior. Believe that the competition cannot tear you down. Believe that you can overcome the negativity and you certainly will.

If you get into a tough situation where doubt clouds your mind, take a moment to step back, breathe deeply and remind yourself that you have the ability. You've trained for this, you are prepared to handle life's hiccups. You are the best and you definitely should not settle for less.

DAY 17
I am beautiful

Beautiful…is not just a song by Snoop Dog featuring Pharrell Williams its the one word we all appreciate being called. The pressure to be physically flawless in our society is damaging our self-worth. The plastic surgery industry keeps growing daily, those who can afford it are sparing no amount to get that perfect model look. Still, with all the money spent on our outer appearance, many feel the need to be model perfect.

The media has created a standard of beauty that is so unrealistic that only a minute fraction of us can attain it. The problem is not that we are all ugly, it's the standards that are unrealistic. Look around you, look deeply at the people you love, your spouse, siblings, parents, children, and friends.

Are they model perfect? Then why do you feel the need to be perfect for them to love you back? You are beautiful irrespective of your flaws. Because it's not just a perfect face that makes you pretty but the light that beams from within you.

Don't put yourself in a miserable state. Studies show that more than 28% of men and 23% of women feel their looks are not good enough.

Sure, young women are more at risk than others, but we all suffer this sad fate. Accept your flaws, instead redirect your mind towards more important issues like taking care of your body by exercising and eating healthy.

Focusing on your physical flaws can have a great impact on your mental health. Studies have shown that beauty obsessed people are more prone to depression and eating disorders. The issue is that thanks to the media, we are all beauty obsessed.

In 2016, Alicia keys started a no makeup revolution to fight back against the unrealistic standards of beauty. This shows that even celebrities worth millions of dollars and a career depending on their looks, do get fed up with living under such pressure.

From billboards to magazines and the movies. We are always reminded of the need to stay perfectly beautiful. Don't give in, fall in love with yourself and not your looks.

People don't like you just because you are beautiful, they love the energy that you bring. Its okay to not be model perfect, its okay to have flaws. You are uniquely beautiful, and no one has any right to determine your right size or shape.

DAY 18

I am strong

Facebook, Instagram, Snapchat and other social media sites are full of pictures and videos showing off their muscles and strength used to lift unimaginable things. This is the 21st century, strength is not about the size of your muscles. It's mental perseverance that matters now.

There are no more lions to be beheaded with your bare hands or bears to wrestle, the struggle now is against your own weakness. Martin Luther King Jr famously said "if you can't fly, then run. If you can't run then walk. If you can't walk, then crawl". Whatever you do never stop because as long as you keep moving, you'll get there.

It's the perseverance of Martin Luther King Jr that help powered the civil rights movement. People always say they want the best life has to offer but they are never willing to do the work. You cannot desire to lose weight and want to spend every waking hour eating massive amounts of sugar filled treats. It does not work that way.

You must be willing to persevere, this is what strength means in modern society. Sure, exercising is very good for your physical and mental health, but when the tribulations of life come, it alone won't help much.

You need your body fit and your mind prepared. Those who choose to take the stairs instead of constantly searching for the easy way out are the true survivors. You too can join the league of high achieving people if you believe that you are strong and force yourself to lift the heavy weight of reality.

Be willing to pay the price for the things you desire and soon they will be yours. Barack Obama's famous speeches are not a natural gift, he practiced until he became very good at it. You too must strengthen your muscles, stop looking for someone to help you.

You are not helpless, you are the only superhero that can save you. Your strength is in your wiliness to never give up. Despite all the pressure and defeat of the civil right movement Dr. King kept persevering. Be fearless, you got this. That goal is not too big for you to conquer. You are more than capable.

DAY 19
I am faithful

When we hear the word faithful, the first thing that comes to our mind is spiritually based. Regardless of your religious views, you probably do not understand how being faithful outside of religion can help rewrite your story. Many people today are eager, they think of a new idea and soon begin chasing the American dream. When difficulty rears its head, they give up.

Being faithful means being steadfast in what you believe. Why then are we not faithful to the things that make us happy? Why are you giving up on that dream of yours because you faced an obstacle?

Despite how you feel in the present, you have to hold on to your dreams. You need to decide to be loyal to yourself. Don't betray your dreams just to fit in and be like everyone else. Your voice deserves a chance to be heard. Jack Ma, the Chinese billionaire, founder, and CEO of Alibaba Group failed at almost everything he tried.

He failed at school, he was rejected as a policeman, KFC refused to hire him, and he was told he will be jailed for starting Alibaba Pay. In leu of of all the obstacles he was faithful to his goal of becoming a success by building the biggest online shopping site in China.

Jack Ma was loyal, are you loyal to that goal that will set you free? It's not okay to just want something you must be willing to hang in there till you get it. You must start strong and finish even stronger.

It's not just about willpower, success is making a deliberate choice to hold on to your dreams and be faithful to those who help you along the way. You too can realize your goals if only you stick to it.

DAY 20
I love myself

I love me, hey
I love me, hey
I don't know about you, but baby
I love
me
Now everybody say, hey-hey-hey
Oh, hey-hey-hey, I love me
Hey-hey-hey, I love me
~ Meghan Trainor ~ I love Me

I love myself as an exceptional individual. There's nobody like me, much the same as there's nobody like you. We may have a lot in common, yet no two individuals are the same. Oscar Wilde profoundly proclaims that "The best romantic tale is simply the one you have".

Love is unconditional, love does not care about imperfections, love conquers all. It's the greatest gift you can give to yourself. Cherish who you are, everything you do and what you keep inside. Your ideas, deformities, struggle, and habits are ours to own.

Loving one's self-goes beyond what you see in the mirror, it's about your identity. Maya Angelo, the historic musician, poet, and activist: had every reason to hate herself, she was raped as a child, the man who rapedher was killed after she told her family about the incidence. She felt guilty and never spoke again.

For the next five years, little Maya denied herself the liberty of her voice, thankfully she found her pride with the help of family. Maya became a woman of grace because she learned to love herself. She forgave any wrongs she thinks she did to herself and embarrassed her imperfect identity.

Sometimes you'll do silly things that make you question your integrity. Things will happen to you that you cannot control. This is not a reason to hate yourself. If you don't love yourself no one else can. "learning to love yourself, it is the greatest love of all" Whitney Houston.

Remember that verse, it's true. You will never meet anyone that will love you as much as you do. Not even your parents, spouse or children can fill the void of self-love. People who lack self-love despise everything they do, they never succeed.

You are special, a unique being, irreplaceable by society. You deserve love, you are accepted just as you are. Never listen to the naysayers, your unconditional love for yourself will calm the storm inside.

DAY 21
I have peace of mind

Peace as defines by Merrium-Webster is:

1. state of tranquility or quiet
2. freedom from disquieting or
3. oppressive thoughts or emotions harmony in personal relations

Peace is calming the subconscious in order to promote harmonious state of well being. The opposite of peace is discord, war and restlessness. All of these dissonate states we have confused for actual productivity. The internet and social media give us the illusion that we are getting things done. Meanwhile, productivity across the country is declining. We stress ourselves every day doing things that don't move us towards our goals.

Social media traps us in a world of instant clicking, deceiving our minds that we are accomplishing important things. Then we lose all strength to focus on the tasks that we really need to do. This kind of behavior pushes our minds into a state of overthinking.

The worst part is that most people are subconsciously deep in worries all the time, but they don't realize it. You are denying your mind of the peace and quietness it needs just to keep up with the Jone's.

You need to take a step back, to a quiet place where you can observe your mind fall into a relaxing state. Yoga and meditation have become a highly sought after skill today because people are trying to escape the bubble of busyness.

Richard Branson often credits his ability to focus on his meditation routines. Oprah Winfrey always starts her day in a quiet room enjoying her thoughts. Overthinking does have a lot of negative impact on our physical and mental well-being. The brain likes making things seem more complicated than they actually are.

You need to take charge of this and keep things as simple as possible. Make plans to get off the internet and spend time alone enjoying your serenity. Peace of mind is not a far-fetched concept but because of the number of stressors and lack of sleep that many suffer, it's becoming increasingly scarce. You oversee your inner peace.

Believe me, there will never be a time when we all will be devoid of concerns at all and that time is death. As long as you're alive there will always be another mountain to climb. Give up control, give up trying to force your mind to do the impossible.

Focus on enjoying peace whenever you can by deliberately scheduling breaks in you day to do so. Don't compromise. You will have peace of mind when you choose to focus on what is in your control. You can push your mind to do incredible things only when you let it rest and regain itself.

DAY 22

I am positive a force

Yes, you are a force to be reckoned with!! Your ideas and gifts are worthy to serve the needs of others. As we journey through this thing called life, we will encounter people and events that try to push us back. We do our best to break through, but we feel overwhelmed. Newton's third law of motion state that "for every action, there is an equal and opposite reaction".

This law goes beyond physics and into everything we do. There will always be those who support you and others who oppose you. Don't panic about this. Its okay for you to have haters. Just know that you are supported. Your ideas are supported. Your dreams are supported.

You are not a coincidence. Its okay to make mistakes. Don't allow the doubts to way you down. Your ideas can help others. Walt Disney was fired for lacking creativity and imagination, yet he went on to build the happiest place on earth.

Our childhood will not be the same without the ideas of Walt Disney. Your dream could have the potential of reshaping the world for the better, why hide it. Now is the time to be that good force, to be the one that people look up to for hope.

Breathe. Know that you are not doing this for you alone. You are fighting a battle for the future generations. Your success will impact people you will never meet. Your fuel tank is full. You can become the person you always desire to be.

We are inspired by others who took the bull by the horn. Be confident in your energy. You will make that impact. You will help your community and you will be a positive presence to reckon with.

DAY 23

I attract positivity

When we think of positivity, our minds focus on ourselves. But it's not just our personal energy that matters, it's the energy in the world around that effect to how we feel. The law of attraction explains that phenomenon the best. We all have a level of frequency we radiate into the world. Others can feel this frequency too. We tend to attract the people on the same frequency with us.

Remember how good it felt to hang out with that friend? That's because they share the same energy as us. Sometimes our family and children can exhibit negative energy. We can divorce our friends, spouse, and jobs but how do you deal with people we deem irreplaceable.

They key is not to tolerate it. Oprah Winfrey tells the story of her family members she had to quit because of negative behavior. When you tolerate the toxic people, more of them will come into your life. You don't have to beat yourself up about getting them to change because it's about you.

Your feelings are in your control. Think about what you're doing or saying that attract these wrong people into your life. If they are family, then find a way to distance yourself from them. They will come to respect your decision and return when they are ready to change.

Be mindful of the energy of others around you because these people can block your positive flow. Warren Buffet advises that we should only keep supportive company because they affect our decisions.

I know it can be hard to accept that your own negative actions and thoughts are attracting toxic people into your life, however, when you accept the truth that you can change your frequency by being more positive, you will break loose. Say these words with me:

I am in charge of my own energy

I am attracting wonderful people into my life

I surround myself with likeminded people

I will not tolerate the negative energy

If someone makes me feel wrong I will not condone it

I know I attract the right people into my life

DAY 24

I am whole

missing in your life, you are not alone. The capitalist economy that we live in has taught us to always want something. It's what drives the economy. Notice the next billboard you see and it will tell you how happier you'll be when you buy their stuff.

But this is an illusion because we have gotten so used to wanting more that many can't seem to see how it's destroying their characters. The insatiable feeling of wanting goes beyond material things, it affects our careers, family, love life, and our inner peace.

We are not satisfied with the way our spouse loves us, worst, we are dissatisfied with our reality. There's never been a better time in human history to be alive. We have more food choices than kings had decades ago. We live longer and safer lives.

We have so much to consume and help us stay productive. Yet, depression is growing at an exponential rate every year. While clinical depression occurs due to chemical imbalances in the brain, most people become depressed because they can't accept the reality of their life. They feel they should be experiencing a better reality.

You can escape this feeling by acknowledging that you are complete. You have all you need to become the person you want to be. On the journey to where you want to be. You appreciate how far you have come.

Don't sacrifice who you are for society's standards. You are a complete being, gifted with everything you need to overcome the adversity. You are not missing strength. You are not missing courage. You have been given all the right people, skills and experience to become your true self.

DAY 25
I am no longer wounded

Everyone at some point in their life will experience a painful event. It could be the loss of family, friends or one's self through abuse like those in the #Metoo movement that spread virally in October 2017. How do we get past these unavoidable sad life events? Well, we cannot ignore them or pray it would not happen to us.

We can let go, allow our self to heal and accept that it happened. Just like our bodies, our souls need time to heal when it has been hurt. The problem is that we keep going back to reopen the wounds. We try to show other people the scars hoping they will empathize with us and not cause us any pain. We harm ourselves because our brains are built to always remember the pain forcing us be "forever victims".

By doing this it ensures you avoid anything that could lead to a repeat of the experience so we think. You can't run away from everyone especially yourself. You cannot hate all men or women because you were victimized. You must let your pain heal and move on.

Charlize Theron the famous actress was wounded from her childhood when her mom shot her alcoholic father. She forged on to try many career pursuits including modeling and ballet dancing, but knee injuries kept dashing her hopes.

She kept going on until she was discovered by a talent manager. She never allowed the trauma of watching the horrible incidence pull her down.

Why are you still holding on to the past? There is nothing you can do to change it. What you remember is only a figment of your imagination because the reality is you have been healed by time. Stop holding on and let go.

Take radical responsibility for your own mind. Remove the victim mentality and focus on the pathology that it has caused in order to gain wholeness.

DAY 26
I am the status quo

The gift of life comes with a bonus of being able to dream. Some people choose not to chase their dreams because they feel that it's impossible to achieve. Don't be like them. Nothing is impossible. I remember sitting at my desk working as a medical biller at a well reknown Insurance company one day just after attending a company meeting. I was called into my boss office and was questioned about a disruption that occurred during that meeting. I was immediately accused, belittled and blamed for the disturbance without having a chance to defend myself or offer any insight to what happened. This event took place during a time in which I was in deep contemplation about going to medical school. I remember returning back to my desk and thinking if this is cooperate America I don't want any parts of it. I'm destined for more.....I want to become a doctor. That day I decided that I would not become any individual who just talked of becoming a doctor but one who would make it happen. You can achieve what you set out to get if you believe and persevere!!!

You are nothing like the others. They may call you crazy, but you know where you're going. Jim Carry suffered poverty in his childhood because his father chose to settle for the status quo, the safe option. His father was an accountant which anyone would think is a safe job, but he was let go when Jim was just 12.

The family had to scramble for whatever they could get to survive. At 16, Jim became a janitor while side hustling as a comedian. The lesson is to not settle for what you think is the safe option. You could make all the safe important life choices and still lose. Why not take the risk to shoot for the stars? If you fail at least you know you gave it your all.

When life gives you an option, never choose the average path. The passion that is burning inside of you is telling you to push harder. You can do much more than many people are willing to work for. Refuse to settle for what others think is the norm.

Be alive. The world needs people who are bold enough to push boundaries. There are no limits in life, there is only illusion because limits are meant to be broken. Even when they say it runs in the family, you can choose to aim higher.

When the pessimist tell you to stop, you forge ahead. These people's minds are limited by what they have chosen. You are the limit. You set the boundaries for yourself and not what society dictates. You can break the chains if only you take charge to become the idol you look up to.

DAY 27
I trust my knowing

One of the most undervalued skills we have is the ability to trust in our guts. We doubt ourselves so much we never take out time to fully comprehend this depth of our knowledge. Malcolm Gladwell in his book *Blink* researches the phenomenon.

Often, we are told that we need to invest a lot of time, effort and money to take a major decision but that's not always the case. The truth is our subconscious mind knows more than we do. It's also faster too. the brain has a fast and slow thinking process. Trusting your knowing also means getting out of your own way.

Stop waiting for a green light before taking actions. Research studies show that when people pauses are monitored, they recognize certain truths earlier than they notice it. What miracle are you waiting for to happen in your life?

Look inside of you and you'll see that you know the answers to the troubles that baffle you. Jeff Bezos, the current richest man in the world started Amazon.com as an online bookshop. As the years went by he followed his instincts and kept expanding the platform.

Amazon is always introducing new products, whether its CreateSpace, their fire devices or the new web services they offer. Jeff trusted that someday things would all pay off. For the first four years of its history, Amazon.com was not a profitable company. Now it's the most valuable company in the world.

Same goes for Facebook's CEO Mark Zuckerberg, he intuitively knew the social media idea was going to be popular with people. Despite knowing he was not going to make money, he kept on reinventing the company until he succeeded.

If you wait for some expert or superhuman to tell you what you need to know then you will never get to your destination. You must take a leap of faith, be assured that your gut will guide you well.

DAY 28

I'm my own person

Dylan McDermott, the lead role actor in the award-winning series "The Practice": has one of the saddest childhood stories I have ever heard. He was born to a 15 years old teenage mother who lived with her boyfriend. Both of them were drug addicts, Dylan never knew his biological father. When he was just 5 years old his mom was murdered by her boyfriend.

His six month old sister was the only family he had left. A few months later, his mom's killer was found dead in the trunk of a car. How could anyone find strength after such events? Studies show that children who experience trauma tend to continue the cycle.

Be that as it may, Dylan transcended that stereotype to become the man he is today. You are your own hero. You cannot depend on someone else to lift the struggles on the inside. Only you can pull through.

DAY 29
I'm above average

Einstein described insanity as doing the same thing over and over again and expecting different results. Many people consider themselves to be normal but what do you call people who repeat the same actions but demand improvement.

Insanity is an overweight people who want to lose weight but keep eating junk food. Or an employee who earns $4000 monthly but wants to earn $13000, yet he does no side hustling. How are you going to get to the things you truly want in life if you never try anything different?

When the Wright brothers were experimenting with their flying machine, people called them crazy. When Srinivasa Ramanujan tried to prove theorems on infinite series they called him crazy. If you are doing what everyone else is, then you will end up like them.

You must do something different if you want to stand out and be above average. What steps are you taking to ensure a different future for yourself? You need to know every decision you make every day will either move you closer or farther from your goals.

Dare to be different. Dare to try something new. Don't settle for average then complain of feeling stuck. If you want that six-figure income, great relationships or extraordinary life, you must be willing to do what the 99% of people are not willing to do.

DAY 30

I accept my greatness

You are the one unavoidable obstacle that is standing in your way. You are capable of doing the things you set out to do. You must trust in yourself and take the initiative. Be committed and consistent with your dreams. The past is gone, the future is not guaranteed, right now, this very moment is what you have.

It's not about what you think or say, it all boils down to what you do. Napster – the origin of filesharing online was created by two teenagers and their uncle: Shawn Parker, Shawn, and John Fanning saw an opportunity to revolutionize the music industry.

They took the initiative, committed all they had to create the social change they desired, and they forced the industry to innovate. Without these guys, we won't have Spotify, iTunes, Pandora and other streaming services today.

Address that fire burning inside of you. You never know the degree of impact you're meant to create. I assure you that when Henry Ford set out to make the car cheap and affordable for all, he never imagined it will revolutionize how the whole world traveled.

He pioneered an industry that is worth over $273 billion today and employs more than two million people according to US statistics. Forget what the negative people will tell you. The successful people going out of their way every day to achieve their goals cannot see the future. They are just like you and I.

The difference is that they choose to believe in their dreams, they decided to give greatness a chance. Lupita Nyong'o was constantly mocked for her dark skin, yet she set out to succeed in an industry where people like her don't go very far.

She had the passion, just like the fire you are experiencing right now. Every great person discovered something unique about themselves and then went for it. J.K Rowling neglected her creative ideas until she had nothing, she found herself on the deep end of life, she gave up control, accepted her ideas and forged on to write one of the best-selling books of all time "Harry Potter" series.

Don't wait till life gives you lemonades to act. There is no use searching for the perfect timing, feelings, and opportunity. Accept your greatness, be brave, go on the journey that only you can conquer. You will pull through, so commit and never give up.

www.ingramcontent.com/pod-product-compliance
Lightning Source LLC
Chambersburg PA
CBHW041526090426
42736CB00035B/30